OBAMACARE LOOPHOLES

Freedom to Not Participate

Michael Vandeburg

The opinions expressed in this book are solely the opinions of the author and do not represent any legal advice, and do not represent the opinions of thoughts of the publisher. The author has represented and warranted full ownership and/or legal right to publish all the materials in this book.

Please be advised that nothing found here has necessarily been reviewed by professionals with the expertise required to provide you with complete, accurate or reliable information.

Not Professional Advice

If you need specific advice (for example, legal, financial, or taxes) please seek a professional who is licensed or knowledgeable in that area.

Obamacare Loopholes: Freedom to Not Participate
All Rights Reserved.

Copyright © 2013 Michael Vandeburg
V1.0

ISBN: 1493772848
ISBN-13: 978-1493772841

ABOUT THE AUTHOR

Michael Vandeburg grew up on a farm just outside of Fort Worth, Texas. He loves to hunt and fish. Growing up in the country and watching his parents work hard to maintain the farm has greatly taught Michael that hard work is very good for the soul. Even now his father still cuts and bails hay in his seventies. Michael has been a contract engineer for over 20 years in the Aerospace, and Truck industries. He is an author / speaker / revivalist, who loves writing to encourage people. Michael's greatest work, and what he wants written on his grave stone one day is, "Author of the Declaration of Independence 2."

Michael has written some very controversial books about taxation rights. Here is a list of his books.

- Income Tax Fraud: Know Your Rights and Liabilities
- Corporate Income Tax: Claim Your Right to Zero Tax Liability in America
- Social Security: The New America Slave
- Why Marijuana is Legal in America
- Walking as Jesus Did (Study Book and Study Guide combined, Audio Book available)
- The Big One Got Away (Children's Short Story about a Fishing Trip, Christian principals, and Audio Book)

Michael has no problem telling the truth, the real problem is no one wants to hear it. The truth convicts, the truth forces you to repent, or continue walking outside of God's will. He is also writing some children's short stories that he hopes will be real encouraging to children.

Praise the Lord always,

Michael

PS: If you loved this book, and love not being yoked in Obamacare, help launch my other books to the New York Times best Seller list. Go to Amazon and order a book.

There is still hope for America!

TABLE OF CONTENTS

ABOUT THE AUTHOR III

CHAPTER 1

    RIGHT OF "FREEDOM NOT TO PARTICIPATE" 1

CHAPTER 2

    UNDER NO DUTY TO ACT 25

CHAPTER 3

    RIGHT OF EXEMPTION IF YOU CANNOT AFFORD COVERAGE 29

CHAPTER 4

    TERM EMPLOYEE BY RIGHT ONLY CORPORATE PERSONS 35

CHAPTER 5

    BY RIGHT PENALTIES ONLY APPLY TO CORPORATE PERSONS 41

CHAPTER 6

    STATES CLAIM RIGHT OF "FREEDOM NOT TO PARTICIPATE" 43

CHAPTER 7

    CLAIM RIGHT OF "TAX EXEMPT STATUS" 49

CHAPTER 8

    CONSTITUTIONAL ISSUES 53

CHAPTER 9

    WHAT SHOULD I DO? 61

CHAPTER 1

RIGHT OF "FREEDOM NOT TO PARTICIPATE"

The first question, are there really any loopholes in Obamacare? These loopholes are based upon my opinion, and I am not giving legal advice.

When evaluating the statutes of Obamacare, or in fact any statutes, the first place I start is looking at what gives it teeth for enforcement, and who does it apply. The more I looked, the more I looked, and looked, and looked, I found no real evidence of any legal power of enforcement within the statutes.

You might be thinking what makes me so sure that there are in fact loopholes? Before I waste everyone's time reading a whole lot of garbage and not proving anything to the masses, let's see if I can immediately come off the bench and cold turkey hit a grand slam, as they call in baseball.

Can I kill this pig right off the bat, or rip one out of the ballpark? Obama is on the mound. He looks to first base, Obama checks the runner! Obama gets another sign from Biden. Obama is looking to home plate, and he is staring down Vandeburg, rearing back he lets it fly, it looks like a 2 seam fastball, whoops it's a hanger folks, will Vandeburg make contact, he did, this one is well hit, it looks, looks, looks, folks it's out of here!!! It hit the water folks! That one was deep out of Wrigley Field. Vandeburg is rounding third and trotting to home plate, the bases are cleared. Is it a grand slam for Vandeburg???

21 **Subtitle G—Miscellaneous**
22 **Provisions**

Page 362
16 **SEC. 1555. FREEDOM NOT TO PARTICIPATE IN FEDERAL**
17 **HEALTH INSURANCE PROGRAMS.**
18 **No individual, company, business, nonprofit entity**, or
19 health insurance issuer offering group or individual health
20 insurance coverage **shall be required to participate** in any
21 Federal health insurance program created under this Act
22 (**or any amendments made by this Act**), or in any Federal
23 health insurance program expanded by this Act (**or any**
24 **such amendments**), and there shall be no penalty or fine

Page 363
1 imposed upon any such issuer for choosing not to partici
2 pate in such programs.

In my humbled opinion I would claim your right to not participate. Then all amendments made by this Act do not apply to you, or me. Can you say little old me? Hey Obama, great slider, but it doesn't apply to me! <u>I claim my freedom to not participate by right</u>. Thank you Obama, but no thanks!!! Amendments include everything within the law, see following amendments list.

No fines, no Obamacare insurance, absolutely nothing of this act will apply to any individual, company, business, or nonprofit entity who claims the right of "Freedom not to Participate". That also means you have the right to continue purchasing your old insurance policy. That also means that Insurance Companies have a legal right to sell the old policies to anyone not participating in Obamacare. If they refuse to sell the old policy to you, I would probably sue them over it. Definitely write them a letter telling them about your rights.

The title of Section 1555 reads almost like no one has the right to freedom until you actually read the section. Maybe that is what threw everyone off from understanding it or reading it. It should have been written "Freedom to not Participate in Federal Health Insurance Programs". It makes me think it was written that way on purpose to confuse everyone. That still doesn't excuse Congress and all the experts who can't read it or understand it. The question has to then be asked did they know about this right and refused to tell everyone?

I would like to say to Nancy Pelosi, that you have to also read it to know what is in it. It appears that no one set down and read all of it. I don't claim to be a genius, I just take the time to read the sections that are really important, and don't get bogged down in all the garbage sections that are meaningless for enforcement. If you do that it doesn't take long to read and understand it.

Obama has been criticized by conservatives for illegally handing out exemptions for Obamacare. The truth is Obama never violated the law. He just withheld the fact that everyone has the same right to complete exemption from the Act by claiming SEC. 1555 FREEDOM NOT TO PARTICIPATE IN FEDERAL HEALTH INSURANCE PROGRAMS.

Personally, I believe Obama has already set a legal precedent for this Section 1555 by handing out all those exemptions. If there would have been a legal issue I think the Republicans would have went after Obama for it, or maybe not. But Obama hasn't violated the Obamacare law.

Maybe you are wondering what are the 'Amendments' made by this Act? That is a very important question encase the IRS was to challenge you. When you go to page one of the Act it starts listing all the amendments of the Act which includes everything within the Act. Below is the list of everything contained in it.

In the Senate of the United States,

December 24, 2009.

Resolved, That the bill from the House of Representatives (H.R. 3590) entitled "An Act to amend the Internal Revenue Code of 1986 to modify the first-time homebuyers credit in the case of members of the Armed Forces and certain other Federal employees, and for other purposes.", do pass with the following

AMENDMENTS:

Strike out all after the enacting clause and insert:

1 SECTION 1. SHORT TITLE; TABLE OF CONTENTS.
2 (a) SHORT TITLE.—This Act may be cited as the "Patient Protection and Affordable Care Act".
4 (b) TABLE OF CONTENTS.—The table of contents of this
5 Act is as follows:
Sec. 1. Short title; table of contents.
TITLE I—QUALITY, AFFORDABLE HEALTH CARE FOR ALL AMERICANS
Subtitle A—Immediate Improvements in Health Care Coverage for All Americans
Sec. 1001. Amendments to the Public Health Service Act.
PART A—INDIVIDUAL AND GROUP MARKET REFORMS
SUBPART II—IMPROVING COVERAGE
Sec. 2711. No lifetime or annual limits.
Sec. 2712. Prohibition on rescissions.
Sec. 2713. Coverage of preventive health services.
Sec. 2714. Extension of dependent coverage.
Sec. 2715. Development and utilization of uniform explanation of coverage documents and standardized definitions.
Sec. 2716. Prohibition of discrimination based on salary.
Sec. 2717. Ensuring the quality of care.
Sec. 2718. Bringing down the cost of health care coverage.
Sec. 2719. Appeals process.
Sec. 1002. Health insurance consumer information.

Sec. 1003. Ensuring that consumers get value for their dollars.
Sec. 1004. Effective dates.
Subtitle B—Immediate Actions to Preserve and Expand Coverage
Sec. 1101. Immediate access to insurance for uninsured individuals with a preexisting condition.
Sec. 1102. Reinsurance for early retirees.
Sec. 1103. Immediate information that allows consumers to identify affordable coverage options.
Sec. 1104. Administrative simplification.
Sec. 1105. Effective date.
Subtitle C—Quality Health Insurance Coverage for All Americans
PART I—HEALTH INSURANCE MARKET REFORMS
Sec. 1201. Amendment to the Public Health Service Act.
SUBPART I—GENERAL REFORM
Sec. 2704. Prohibition of preexisting condition exclusions or other discrimination based on health status.
Sec. 2701. Fair health insurance premiums.
Sec. 2702. Guaranteed availability of coverage.
Sec. 2703. Guaranteed renewability of coverage.
Sec. 2705. Prohibiting discrimination against individual participants and beneficiaries based on health status.
Sec. 2706. Non-discrimination in health care.
Sec. 2707. Comprehensive health insurance coverage.
Sec. 2708. Prohibition on excessive waiting periods.
PART II—OTHER PROVISIONS
Sec. 1251. Preservation of right to maintain existing coverage.
Sec. 1252. Rating reforms must apply uniformly to all health insurance issuers and group health plans.
Sec. 1253. Effective dates.
Subtitle D—Available Coverage Choices for All Americans
PART I—ESTABLISHMENT OF QUALIFIED HEALTH PLANS
Sec. 1301. Qualified health plan defined.
Sec. 1302. Essential health benefits requirements.
Sec. 1303. Special rules.
Sec. 1304. Related definitions.
PART II—CONSUMER CHOICES AND INSURANCE COMPETITION THROUGH HEALTH BENEFIT EXCHANGES
Sec. 1311. Affordable choices of health benefit plans.
Sec. 1312. Consumer choice.
Sec. 1313. Financial integrity.

PART III—STATE FLEXIBILITY RELATING TO EXCHANGES
Sec. 1321. State flexibility in operation and enforcement of Exchanges and related requirements.
Sec. 1322. Federal program to assist establishment and operation of nonprofit,member-run health insurance issuers.
Sec. 1323. Community health insurance option.
Sec. 1324. Level playing field.
PART IV—STATE FLEXIBILITY TO ESTABLISH ALTERNATIVE PROGRAMS
Sec. 1331. State flexibility to establish basic health programs for low-income individuals not eligible for Medicaid.
Sec. 1332. Waiver for State innovation.
Sec. 1333. Provisions relating to offering of plans in more than one State.
PART V—REINSURANCE AND RISK ADJUSTMENT
Sec. 1341. Transitional reinsurance program for individual and small group markets in each State.
Sec. 1342. Establishment of risk corridors for plans in individual and small group markets.
Sec. 1343. Risk adjustment.
Subtitle E—Affordable Coverage Choices for All Americans
PART I—PREMIUM TAX CREDITS AND COST-SHARING REDUCTIONS
SUBPART A—PREMIUM TAX CREDITS AND COST-SHARING REDUCTIONS
Sec. 1401. Refundable tax credit providing premium assistance for coverage under a qualified health plan.
Sec. 1402. Reduced cost-sharing for individuals enrolling in qualified health plans.
SUBPART B—ELIGIBILITY DETERMINATIONS
Sec. 1411. Procedures for determining eligibility for Exchange participation, premium tax credits and reduced cost-sharing, and individual responsibility exemptions.
Sec. 1412. Advance determination and payment of premium tax credits and costsharing reductions.
Sec. 1413. Streamlining of procedures for enrollment through an exchange and State Medicaid, CHIP, and health subsidy programs.
Sec. 1414. Disclosures to carry out eligibility requirements for certain programs.
Sec. 1415. Premium tax credit and cost-sharing reduction payments disregarded for Federal and Federally-assisted programs.
PART II—SMALL BUSINESS TAX CREDIT
Sec. 1421. Credit for employee health insurance expenses of small businesses.

Subtitle F—Shared Responsibility for Health Care
PART I—INDIVIDUAL RESPONSIBILITY
Sec. 1501. Requirement to maintain minimum essential coverage.
Sec. 1502. Reporting of health insurance coverage.
PART II—EMPLOYER RESPONSIBILITIES
Sec. 1511. Automatic enrollment for employees of large employers.
Sec. 1512. Employer requirement to inform employees of coverage options.
Sec. 1513. Shared responsibility for employers.
Sec. 1514. Reporting of employer health insurance coverage.
Sec. 1515. Offering of Exchange-participating qualified health plans through cafeteria plans.
Subtitle G—Miscellaneous Provisions
Sec. 1551. Definitions.
Sec. 1552. Transparency in government.
Sec. 1553. Prohibition against discrimination on assisted suicide.
Sec. 1554. Access to therapies.
Sec. 1555. Freedom not to participate in Federal health insurance programs.
Sec. 1556. Equity for certain eligible survivors.
Sec. 1557. Nondiscrimination.
Sec. 1558. Protections for employees.
Sec. 1559. Oversight.
Sec. 1560. Rules of construction.
Sec. 1561. Health information technology enrollment standards and protocols.
Sec. 1562. Conforming amendments.
Sec. 1563. Sense of the Senate promoting fiscal responsibility.
TITLE II—ROLE OF PUBLIC PROGRAMS
Subtitle A—Improved Access to Medicaid
Sec. 2001. Medicaid coverage for the lowest income populations.
Sec. 2002. Income eligibility for nonelderly determined using modified gross income.
Sec. 2003. Requirement to offer premium assistance for employer-sponsored insurance.
Sec. 2004. Medicaid coverage for former foster care children.
Sec. 2005. Payments to territories.
Sec. 2006. Special adjustment to FMAP determination for certain States recovering from a major disaster.
Sec. 2007. Medicaid Improvement Fund rescission.

Subtitle B—Enhanced Support for the Children's Health Insurance Program
Sec. 2101. Additional federal financial participation for CHIP.
Sec. 2102. Technical corrections.
Subtitle C—Medicaid and CHIP Enrollment Simplification
Sec. 2201. Enrollment Simplification and coordination with State Health Insurance Exchanges.
Sec. 2202. Permitting hospitals to make presumptive eligibility determinations for all Medicaid eligible populations.
Subtitle D—Improvements to Medicaid Services
Sec. 2301. Coverage for freestanding birth center services.
Sec. 2302. Concurrent care for children.
Sec. 2303. State eligibility option for family planning services.
Sec. 2304. Clarification of definition of medical assistance.
Subtitle E—New Options for States to Provide Long-Term Services and Supports
Sec. 2401. Community First Choice Option.
Sec. 2402. Removal of barriers to providing home and community-based services.
Sec. 2403. Money Follows the Person Rebalancing Demonstration.
Sec. 2404. Protection for recipients of home and community-based services against spousal impoverishment.
Sec. 2405. Funding to expand State Aging and Disability Resource Centers.
Sec. 2406. Sense of the Senate regarding long-term care.
Subtitle F—Medicaid Prescription Drug Coverage
Sec. 2501. Prescription drug rebates.
Sec. 2502. Elimination of exclusion of coverage of certain drugs.
Sec. 2503. Providing adequate pharmacy reimbursement.
Subtitle G—Medicaid Disproportionate Share Hospital (DSH) Payments
Sec. 2551. Disproportionate share hospital payments.
Subtitle H—Improved Coordination for Dual Eligible Beneficiaries
Sec. 2601. 5-year period for demonstration projects.
Sec. 2602. Providing Federal coverage and payment coordination for dual eligible beneficiaries.
Subtitle I—Improving the Quality of Medicaid for Patients and Providers
Sec. 2701. Adult health quality measures.
Sec. 2702. Payment Adjustment for Health Care-Acquired Conditions.
Sec. 2703. State option to provide health homes for enrollees with chronic conditions.

Sec. 2704. Demonstration project to evaluate integrated care around a hospitalization.
Sec. 2705. Medicaid Global Payment System Demonstration Project.
Sec. 2706. Pediatric Accountable Care Organization Demonstration Project.
Sec. 2707. Medicaid emergency psychiatric demonstration project.
Subtitle J—Improvements to the Medicaid and CHIP Payment and Access Commission (MACPAC)
Sec. 2801. MACPAC assessment of policies affecting all Medicaid beneficiaries.Subtitle K—Protections for American Indians and Alaska Natives
Sec. 2901. Special rules relating to Indians.
Sec. 2902. Elimination of sunset for reimbursement for all medicare part B services furnished by certain indian hospitals and clinics.
Subtitle L—Maternal and Child Health Services
Sec. 2951. Maternal, infant, and early childhood home visiting programs.
Sec. 2952. Support, education, and research for postpartum depression.
Sec. 2953. Personal responsibility education.
Sec. 2954. Restoration of funding for abstinence education.
Sec. 2955. Inclusion of information about the importance of having a health care power of attorney in transition planning for children aging out of foster care and independent living programs.
TITLE III—IMPROVING THE QUALITY AND EFFICIENCY OF HEALTH CARE
Subtitle A—Transforming the Health Care Delivery System
PART I—LINKING PAYMENT TO QUALITY OUTCOMES UNDER THE MEDICARE PROGRAM
Sec. 3001. Hospital Value-Based purchasing program.
Sec. 3002. Improvements to the physician quality reporting system.
Sec. 3003. Improvements to the physician feedback program.
Sec. 3004. Quality reporting for long-term care hospitals, inpatient rehabilitation hospitals, and hospice programs.
Sec. 3005. Quality reporting for PPS-exempt cancer hospitals.
Sec. 3006. Plans for a Value-Based purchasing program for skilled nursing facilities and home health agencies.
Sec. 3007. Value-based payment modifier under the physician fee schedule.
Sec. 3008. Payment adjustment for conditions acquired in hospitals.
PART II—NATIONAL STRATEGY TO IMPROVE HEALTH CARE QUALITY
Sec. 3011. National strategy.
Sec. 3012. Interagency Working Group on Health Care Quality.

Sec. 3013. Quality measure development.
Sec. 3014. Quality measurement.
Sec. 3015. Data collection; public reporting.
PART III—ENCOURAGING DEVELOPMENT OF NEW PATIENT CARE MODELS
Sec. 3021. Establishment of Center for Medicare and Medicaid Innovation within CMS.
Sec. 3022. Medicare shared savings program.
Sec. 3023. National pilot program on payment bundling.
Sec. 3024. Independence at home demonstration program.
Sec. 3025. Hospital readmissions reduction program.
Sec. 3026. Community-Based Care Transitions Program.
Sec. 3027. Extension of gainsharing demonstration.
Subtitle B—Improving Medicare for Patients and Providers
PART I—ENSURING BENEFICIARY ACCESS TO PHYSICIAN CARE AND OTHER SERVICES
Sec. 3101. Increase in the physician payment update.
Sec. 3102. Extension of the work geographic index floor and revisions to the practice expense geographic adjustment under the Medicare physician fee schedule.
Sec. 3103. Extension of exceptions process for Medicare therapy caps.
Sec. 3104. Extension of payment for technical component of certain physician pathology services.
Sec. 3105. Extension of ambulance add-ons.
Sec. 3106. Extension of certain payment rules for long-term care hospital services and of moratorium on the establishment of certain hospitals and facilities.
Sec. 3107. Extension of physician fee schedule mental health add-on.
Sec. 3108. Permitting physician assistants to order post-Hospital extended care services.
Sec. 3109. Exemption of certain pharmacies from accreditation requirements.
Sec. 3110. Part B special enrollment period for disabled TRICARE beneficiaries.
Sec. 3111. Payment for bone density tests.
Sec. 3112. Revision to the Medicare Improvement Fund.
Sec. 3113. Treatment of certain complex diagnostic laboratory tests.
Sec. 3114. Improved access for certified nurse-midwife services.
PART II—RURAL PROTECTIONS
Sec. 3121. Extension of outpatient hold harmless provision.

Sec. 3122. Extension of Medicare reasonable costs payments for certain clinical diagnostic laboratory tests furnished to hospital patients in certain rural areas.
Sec. 3123. Extension of the Rural Community Hospital Demonstration Program.
Sec. 3124. Extension of the Medicare-dependent hospital (MDH) program.
Sec. 3125. Temporary improvements to the Medicare inpatient hospital payment adjustment for low-volume hospitals.
Sec. 3126. Improvements to the demonstration project on community health integration models in certain rural counties.
Sec. 3127. MedPAC study on adequacy of Medicare payments for health care providers serving in rural areas.
Sec. 3128. Technical correction related to critical access hospital services.
Sec. 3129. Extension of and revisions to Medicare rural hospital flexibility program.
PART III—IMPROVING PAYMENT ACCURACY
Sec. 3131. Payment adjustments for home health care.
Sec. 3132. Hospice reform.
Sec. 3133. Improvement to medicare disproportionate share hospital (DSH) payments.
Sec. 3134. Misvalued codes under the physician fee schedule.
Sec. 3135. Modification of equipment utilization factor for advanced imaging services.
Sec. 3136. Revision of payment for power-driven wheelchairs.
Sec. 3137. Hospital wage index improvement.
Sec. 3138. Treatment of certain cancer hospitals.
Sec. 3139. Payment for biosimilar biological products.
Sec. 3140. Medicare hospice concurrent care demonstration program.
Sec. 3141. Application of budget neutrality on a national basis in the calculation of the Medicare hospital wage index floor.
Sec. 3142. HHS study on urban Medicare-dependent hospitals.
Sec. 3143. Protecting home health benefits.
Subtitle C—Provisions Relating to Part C
Sec. 3201. Medicare Advantage payment.
Sec. 3202. Benefit protection and simplification.
Sec. 3203. Application of coding intensity adjustment during MA payment transition.
Sec. 3204. Simplification of annual beneficiary election periods.
Sec. 3205. Extension for specialized MA plans for special needs individuals.

Sec. 3206. Extension of reasonable cost contracts.
Sec. 3207. Technical correction to MA private fee-for-service plans.
Sec. 3208. Making senior housing facility demonstration permanent.
Sec. 3209. Authority to deny plan bids.
Sec. 3210. Development of new standards for certain Medigap plans.
Subtitle D—Medicare Part D Improvements for Prescription Drug Plans and MA–PD Plans
Sec. 3301. Medicare coverage gap discount program.
Sec. 3302. Improvement in determination of Medicare part D low-income benchmark premium.
Sec. 3303. Voluntary de minimis policy for subsidy eligible individuals under prescription drug plans and MA–PD plans.
Sec. 3304. Special rule for widows and widowers regarding eligibility for low-income assistance.
Sec. 3305. Improved information for subsidy eligible individuals reassigned to prescription drug plans and MA–PD plans.
Sec. 3306. Funding outreach and assistance for low-income programs.
Sec. 3307. Improving formulary requirements for prescription drug plans and MA–PD plans with respect to certain categories or classes of drugs.
Sec. 3308. Reducing part D premium subsidy for high-income beneficiaries.
Sec. 3309. Elimination of cost sharing for certain dual eligible individuals.
Sec. 3310. Reducing wasteful dispensing of outpatient prescription drugs in longterm care facilities under prescription drug plans and MA–PD plans.
Sec. 3311. Improved Medicare prescription drug plan and MA–PD plan complaint system.
Sec. 3312. Uniform exceptions and appeals process for prescription drug plans and MA–PD plans.
Sec. 3313. Office of the Inspector General studies and reports.
Sec. 3314. Including costs incurred by AIDS drug assistance programs and Indian Health Service in providing prescription drugs toward the annual out-of-pocket threshold under part D.
Sec. 3315. Immediate reduction in coverage gap in 2010.
Subtitle E—Ensuring Medicare Sustainability
Sec. 3401. Revision of certain market basket updates and incorporation of productivity improvements into market basket updates that do not already incorporate such improvements.
Sec. 3402. Temporary adjustment to the calculation of part B premiums.
Sec. 3403. Independent Medicare Advisory Board.
Subtitle F—Health Care Quality Improvements

Sec. 3501. Health care delivery system research; Quality improvement technical assistance.
Sec. 3502. Establishing community health teams to support the patient-centered medical home.
Sec. 3503. Medication management services in treatment of chronic disease.
Sec. 3504. Design and implementation of regionalized systems for emergency care.
Sec. 3505. Trauma care centers and service availability.
Sec. 3506. Program to facilitate shared decisionmaking.
Sec. 3507. Presentation of prescription drug benefit and risk information.
Sec. 3508. Demonstration program to integrate quality improvement and patient safety training into clinical education of health professionals.
Sec. 3509. Improving women's health.
Sec. 3510. Patient navigator program.
Sec. 3511. Authorization of appropriations.
Subtitle G—Protecting and Improving Guaranteed Medicare Benefits
Sec. 3601. Protecting and improving guaranteed Medicare benefits.
Sec. 3602. No cuts in guaranteed benefits.
TITLE IV—PREVENTION OF CHRONIC DISEASE AND IMPROVING PUBLIC HEALTH
Subtitle A—Modernizing Disease Prevention and Public Health Systems
Sec. 4001. National Prevention, Health Promotion and Public Health Council.
Sec. 4002. Prevention and Public Health Fund.
Sec. 4003. Clinical and community preventive services.
Sec. 4004. Education and outreach campaign regarding preventive benefits.
Subtitle B—Increasing Access to Clinical Preventive Services
Sec. 4101. School-based health centers.
Sec. 4102. Oral healthcare prevention activities.
Sec. 4103. Medicare coverage of annual wellness visit providing a personalized prevention plan.
Sec. 4104. Removal of barriers to preventive services in Medicare.
Sec. 4105. Evidence-based coverage of preventive services in Medicare.
Sec. 4106. Improving access to preventive services for eligible adults in Medicaid.
Sec. 4107. Coverage of comprehensive tobacco cessation services for pregnant women in Medicaid.
Sec. 4108. Incentives for prevention of chronic diseases in medicaid.

Subtitle C—Creating Healthier Communities
Sec. 4201. Community transformation grants.
Sec. 4202. Healthy aging, living well; evaluation of community-based prevention and wellness programs for Medicare beneficiaries.
Sec. 4203. Removing barriers and improving access to wellness for individuals with disabilities.
Sec. 4204. Immunizations.
Sec. 4205. Nutrition labeling of standard menu items at chain restaurants.
Sec. 4206. Demonstration project concerning individualized wellness plan.
Sec. 4207. Reasonable break time for nursing mothers.
Subtitle D—Support for Prevention and Public Health Innovation
Sec. 4301. Research on optimizing the delivery of public health services.
Sec. 4302. Understanding health disparities: data collection and analysis.
Sec. 4303. CDC and employer-based wellness programs.
Sec. 4304. Epidemiology-Laboratory Capacity Grants.
Sec. 4305. Advancing research and treatment for pain care management.
Sec. 4306. Funding for Childhood Obesity Demonstration Project.
Subtitle E—Miscellaneous Provisions
Sec. 4401. Sense of the Senate concerning CBO scoring.
Sec. 4402. Effectiveness of Federal health and wellness initiatives.
TITLE V—HEALTH CARE WORKFORCE
Subtitle A—Purpose and Definitions
Sec. 5001. Purpose.
Sec. 5002. Definitions.
Subtitle B—Innovations in the Health Care Workforce
Sec. 5101. National health care workforce commission.
Sec. 5102. State health care workforce development grants.
Sec. 5103. Health care workforce assessment.
Subtitle C—Increasing the Supply of the Health Care Workforce
Sec. 5201. Federally supported student loan funds.
Sec. 5202. Nursing student loan program.
Sec. 5203. Health care workforce loan repayment programs.
Sec. 5204. Public health workforce recruitment and retention programs.
Sec. 5205. Allied health workforce recruitment and retention programs.
Sec. 5206. Grants for State and local programs.
Sec. 5207. Funding for National Health Service Corps.
Sec. 5208. Nurse-managed health clinics.
Sec. 5209. Elimination of cap on commissioned corps.
Sec. 5210. Establishing a Ready Reserve Corps.
Subtitle D—Enhancing Health Care Workforce Education and Training

Sec. 5301. Training in family medicine, general internal medicine, general pediatrics,and physician assistantship.
Sec. 5302. Training opportunities for direct care workers.
Sec. 5303. Training in general, pediatric, and public health dentistry.
Sec. 5304. Alternative dental health care providers demonstration project.
Sec. 5305. Geriatric education and training; career awards; comprehensive geriatric education.
Sec. 5306. Mental and behavioral health education and training grants.
Sec. 5307. Cultural competency, prevention, and public health and individuals with disabilities training.
Sec. 5308. Advanced nursing education grants.
Sec. 5309. Nurse education, practice, and retention grants.
Sec. 5310. Loan repayment and scholarship program.
Sec. 5311. Nurse faculty loan program.
Sec. 5312. Authorization of appropriations for parts B through D of title VIII.
Sec. 5313. Grants to promote the community health workforce.
Sec. 5314. Fellowship training in public health.
Sec. 5315. United States Public Health Sciences Track.
Subtitle E—Supporting the Existing Health Care Workforce
Sec. 5401. Centers of excellence.
Sec. 5402. Health care professionals training for diversity.
Sec. 5403. Interdisciplinary, community-based linkages.
Sec. 5404. Workforce diversity grants.
Sec. 5405. Primary care extension program.
Subtitle F—Strengthening Primary Care and Other Workforce Improvements
Sec. 5501. Expanding access to primary care services and general surgery services.
Sec. 5502. Medicare Federally qualified health center improvements.
Sec. 5503. Distribution of additional residency positions.
Sec. 5504. Counting resident time in nonprovider settings.
Sec. 5505. Rules for counting resident time for didactic and scholarly activities and other activities.
Sec. 5506. Preservation of resident cap positions from closed hospitals.
Sec. 5507. Demonstration projects To address health professions workforce needs;
extension of family-to-family health information centers.
Sec. 5508. Increasing teaching capacity.
Sec. 5509. Graduate nurse education demonstration.

Subtitle G—Improving Access to Health Care Services
Sec. 5601. Spending for Federally Qualified Health Centers (FQHCs).
Sec. 5602. Negotiated rulemaking for development of methodology and criteria for designating medically underserved populations and health professions shortage areas.
Sec. 5603. Reauthorization of the Wakefield Emergency Medical Services for Children Program.
Sec. 5604. Co-locating primary and specialty care in community-based mental health settings.
Sec. 5605. Key National indicators.
Subtitle H—General Provisions
Sec. 5701. Reports.
TITLE VI—TRANSPARENCY AND PROGRAM INTEGRITY
Subtitle A—Physician Ownership and Other Transparency
Sec. 6001. Limitation on Medicare exception to the prohibition on certain physician referrals for hospitals.
Sec. 6002. Transparency reports and reporting of physician ownership or investment interests.
Sec. 6003. Disclosure requirements for in-office ancillary services exception to the prohibition on physician self-referral for certain imaging services.
Sec. 6004. Prescription drug sample transparency.
Sec. 6005. Pharmacy benefit managers transparency requirements.
Subtitle B—Nursing Home Transparency and Improvement
PART I—IMPROVING TRANSPARENCY OF INFORMATION
Sec. 6101. Required disclosure of ownership and additional disclosable parties information.
Sec. 6102. Accountability requirements for skilled nursing facilities and nursing facilities.
Sec. 6103. Nursing home compare Medicare website.
Sec. 6104. Reporting of expenditures.
Sec. 6105. Standardized complaint form.
Sec. 6106. Ensuring staffing accountability.
Sec. 6107. GAO study and report on Five-Star Quality Rating System.
PART II—TARGETING ENFORCEMENT
Sec. 6111. Civil money penalties.
Sec. 6112. National independent monitor demonstration project.
Sec. 6113. Notification of facility closure.
Sec. 6114. National demonstration projects on culture change and use of information technology in nursing homes.

PART III—IMPROVING STAFF TRAINING
Sec. 6121. Dementia and abuse prevention training.
Subtitle C—Nationwide Program for National and State Background Checks on Direct Patient Access Employees of Long-term Care Facilities and Providers
Sec. 6201. Nationwide program for National and State background checks on direct patient access employees of long-term care facilities and providers.
Subtitle D—Patient-Centered Outcomes Research
Sec. 6301. Patient-Centered Outcomes Research.
Sec. 6302. Federal coordinating council for comparative effectiveness research.
Subtitle E—Medicare, Medicaid, and CHIP Program Integrity Provisions
Sec. 6401. Provider screening and other enrollment requirements under Medicare,Medicaid, and CHIP.
Sec. 6402. Enhanced Medicare and Medicaid program integrity provisions.
Sec. 6403. Elimination of duplication between the Healthcare Integrity and Protection Data Bank and the National Practitioner Data Bank.
Sec. 6404. Maximum period for submission of Medicare claims reduced to not more than 12 months.
Sec. 6405. Physicians who order items or services required to be Medicare enrolled physicians or eligible professionals.
Sec. 6406. Requirement for physicians to provide documentation on referrals to programs at high risk of waste and abuse.
Sec. 6407. Face to face encounter with patient required before physicians may certify eligibility for home health services or durable medical equipment under Medicare.
Sec. 6408. Enhanced penalties.
Sec. 6409. Medicare self-referral disclosure protocol.
Sec. 6410. Adjustments to the Medicare durable medical equipment, prosthetics,orthotics, and supplies competitive acquisition program.
Sec. 6411. Expansion of the Recovery Audit Contractor (RAC) program.
Subtitle F—Additional Medicaid Program Integrity Provisions
Sec. 6501. Termination of provider participation under Medicaid if terminated under Medicare or other State plan.
Sec. 6502. Medicaid exclusion from participation relating to certain ownership,control, and management affiliations.
Sec. 6503. Billing agents, clearinghouses, or other alternate payees required to register under Medicaid.

Sec. 6504. Requirement to report expanded set of data elements under MMIS to detect fraud and abuse.
Sec. 6505. Prohibition on payments to institutions or entities located outside of the United States.
Sec. 6506. Overpayments.
Sec. 6507. Mandatory State use of national correct coding initiative.
Sec. 6508. General effective date.
Subtitle G—Additional Program Integrity Provisions
Sec. 6601. Prohibition on false statements and representations.
Sec. 6602. Clarifying definition.
Sec. 6603. Development of model uniform report form.
Sec. 6604. Applicability of State law to combat fraud and abuse.
Sec. 6605. Enabling the Department of Labor to issue administrative summary cease and desist orders and summary seizures orders against plans that are in financially hazardous condition.
Sec. 6606. MEWA plan registration with Department of Labor.
Sec. 6607. Permitting evidentiary privilege and confidential communications.
Subtitle H—Elder Justice Act
Sec. 6701. Short title of subtitle.
Sec. 6702. Definitions.
Sec. 6703. Elder Justice.
Subtitle I—Sense of the Senate Regarding Medical Malpractice
Sec. 6801. Sense of the Senate regarding medical malpractice.
TITLE VII—IMPROVING ACCESS TO INNOVATIVE MEDICAL THERAPIES
Subtitle A—Biologics Price Competition and Innovation
Sec. 7001. Short title.
Sec. 7002. Approval pathway for biosimilar biological products.
Sec. 7003. Savings.
Subtitle B—More Affordable Medicines for Children and Underserved Communities
Sec. 7101. Expanded participation in 340B program.
Sec. 7102. Improvements to 340B program integrity.
Sec. 7103. GAO study to make recommendations on improving the 340B program.
TITLE VIII—CLASS ACT
Sec. 8001. Short title of title.
Sec. 8002. Establishment of national voluntary insurance program for purchasing community living assistance services and support.
TITLE IX—REVENUE PROVISIONS

Subtitle A—Revenue Offset Provisions
Sec. 9001. Excise tax on high cost employer-sponsored health coverage.
Sec. 9002. Inclusion of cost of employer-sponsored health coverage on W–2.
Sec. 9003. Distributions for medicine qualified only if for prescribed drug or insulin.
Sec. 9004. Increase in additional tax on distributions from HSAs and Archer MSAs not used for qualified medical expenses.
Sec. 9005. Limitation on health flexible spending arrangements under cafeteria plans.
Sec. 9006. Expansion of information reporting requirements.
Sec. 9007. Additional requirements for charitable hospitals.
Sec. 9008. Imposition of annual fee on branded prescription pharmaceutical manufacturers and importers.
Sec. 9009. Imposition of annual fee on medical device manufacturers and importers.
Sec. 9010. Imposition of annual fee on health insurance providers.
Sec. 9011. Study and report of effect on veterans health care.
Sec. 9012. Elimination of deduction for expenses allocable to Medicare Part D subsidy.
Sec. 9013. Modification of itemized deduction for medical expenses.
Sec. 9014. Limitation on excessive remuneration paid by certain health insurance providers.
Sec. 9015. Additional hospital insurance tax on high-income taxpayers.
Sec. 9016. Modification of section 833 treatment of certain health organizations.
Sec. 9017. Excise tax on elective cosmetic medical procedures.
Subtitle B—Other Provisions
Sec. 9021. Exclusion of health benefits provided by Indian tribal governments.
Sec. 9022. Establishment of simple cafeteria plans for small businesses.
Sec. 9023. Qualifying therapeutic discovery project credit.
TITLE X—STRENGTHENING QUALITY, AFFORDABLE HEALTH CARE FOR ALL AMERICANS
Subtitle A—Provisions Relating to Title I
Sec. 10101. Amendments to subtitle A.
Sec. 10102. Amendments to subtitle B.
Sec. 10103. Amendments to subtitle C.
Sec. 10104. Amendments to subtitle D.
Sec. 10105. Amendments to subtitle E.

Sec. 10106. Amendments to subtitle F.
Sec. 10107. Amendments to subtitle G.
Sec. 10108. Free choice vouchers.
Sec. 10109. Development of standards for financial and administrative transactions.
Subtitle B—Provisions Relating to Title II
PART I—MEDICAID AND CHIP
Sec. 10201. Amendments to the Social Security Act and title II of this Act.
Sec. 10202. Incentives for States to offer home and community-based services as a long-term care alternative to nursing homes.
Sec. 10203. Extension of funding for CHIP through fiscal year 2015 and other CHIP-related provisions.
PART II—SUPPORT FOR PREGNANT AND PARENTING TEENS AND WOMEN
Sec. 10211. Definitions.
Sec. 10212. Establishment of pregnancy assistance fund.
Sec. 10213. Permissible uses of Fund.
Sec. 10214. Appropriations.
PART III—INDIAN HEALTH CARE IMPROVEMENT
Sec. 10221. Indian health care improvement.
Subtitle C—Provisions Relating to Title III
Sec. 10301. Plans for a Value-Based purchasing program for ambulatory surgical centers.
Sec. 10302. Revision to national strategy for quality improvement in health care.
Sec. 10303. Development of outcome measures.
Sec. 10304. Selection of efficiency measures.
Sec. 10305. Data collection; public reporting.
Sec. 10306. Improvements under the Center for Medicare and Medicaid Innovation.
Sec. 10307. Improvements to the Medicare shared savings program.
Sec. 10308. Revisions to national pilot program on payment bundling.
Sec. 10309. Revisions to hospital readmissions reduction program.
Sec. 10310. Repeal of physician payment update.
Sec. 10311. Revisions to extension of ambulance add-ons.
Sec. 10312. Certain payment rules for long-term care hospital services and moratorium on the establishment of certain hospitals and facilities.
Sec. 10313. Revisions to the extension for the rural community hospital demonstration program.
Sec. 10314. Adjustment to low-volume hospital provision.
Sec. 10315. Revisions to home health care provisions.

Sec. 10316. Medicare DSH.
Sec. 10317. Revisions to extension of section 508 hospital provisions.
Sec. 10318. Revisions to transitional extra benefits under Medicare Advantage.
Sec. 10319. Revisions to market basket adjustments.
Sec. 10320. Expansion of the scope of, and additional improvements to, the Independent Medicare Advisory Board.
Sec. 10321. Revision to community health teams.
Sec. 10322. Quality reporting for psychiatric hospitals.
Sec. 10323. Medicare coverage for individuals exposed to environmental health hazards.
Sec. 10324. Protections for frontier States.
Sec. 10325. Revision to skilled nursing facility prospective payment system.
Sec. 10326. Pilot testing pay-for-performance programs for certain Medicare providers.
Sec. 10327. Improvements to the physician quality reporting system.
Sec. 10328. Improvement in part D medication therapy management (MTM) programs.
Sec. 10329. Developing methodology to assess health plan value.
Sec. 10330. Modernizing computer and data systems of the Centers for Medicare & Medicaid services to support improvements in care delivery.
Sec. 10331. Public reporting of performance information.
Sec. 10332. Availability of medicare data for performance measurement.
Sec. 10333. Community-based collaborative care networks.
Sec. 10334. Minority health.
Sec. 10335. Technical correction to the hospital value-based purchasing program.
Sec. 10336. GAO study and report on Medicare beneficiary access to high-quality dialysis services.
Subtitle D—Provisions Relating to Title IV
Sec. 10401. Amendments to subtitle A.
Sec. 10402. Amendments to subtitle B.
Sec. 10403. Amendments to subtitle C.
Sec. 10404. Amendments to subtitle D.
Sec. 10405. Amendments to subtitle E.
Sec. 10406. Amendment relating to waiving coinsurance for preventive services.
Sec. 10407. Better diabetes care.

Sec. 10408. Grants for small businesses to provide comprehensive workplace wellness programs.
Sec. 10409. Cures Acceleration Network.
Sec. 10410. Centers of Excellence for Depression.
Sec. 10411. Programs relating to congenital heart disease.
Sec. 10412. Automated Defibrillation in Adam's Memory Act.
Sec. 10413. Young women's breast health awareness and support of young women diagnosed with breast cancer.
Subtitle E—Provisions Relating to Title V
Sec. 10501. Amendments to the Public Health Service Act, the Social Security Act, and title V of this Act.
Sec. 10502. Infrastructure to Expand Access to Care.
Sec. 10503. Community Health Centers and the National Health Service Corps Fund.
Sec. 10504. Demonstration project to provide access to affordable care.
Subtitle F—Provisions Relating to Title VI
Sec. 10601. Revisions to limitation on medicare exception to the prohibition on certain physician referrals for hospitals.
Sec. 10602. Clarifications to patient-centered outcomes research.
Sec. 10603. Striking provisions relating to individual provider application fees.
Sec. 10604. Technical correction to section 6405.
Sec. 10605. Certain other providers permitted to conduct face to face encounter for home health services.
Sec. 10606. Health care fraud enforcement.
Sec. 10607. State demonstration programs to evaluate alternatives to current medical tort litigation.
Sec. 10608. Extension of medical malpractice coverage to free clinics.
Sec. 10609. Labeling changes.
Subtitle G—Provisions Relating to Title VIII
Sec. 10801. Provisions relating to title VIII.
Subtitle H—Provisions Relating to Title IX
Sec. 10901. Modifications to excise tax on high cost employer-sponsored health coverage.
Sec. 10902. Inflation adjustment of limitation on health flexible spending arrangements under cafeteria plans.
Sec. 10903. Modification of limitation on charges by charitable hospitals.
Sec. 10904. Modification of annual fee on medical device manufacturers and importers.
Sec. 10905. Modification of annual fee on health insurance providers.

Sec. 10906. Modifications to additional hospital insurance tax on high-income taxpayers.
Sec. 10907. Excise tax on indoor tanning services in lieu of elective cosmetic medical
procedures.
Sec. 10908. Exclusion for assistance provided to participants in State student
loan repayment programs for certain health professionals.
Sec. 10909. Expansion of adoption credit and adoption assistance programs.

As you can read the entire Act is made up of Amendments. That means that if you claim your "right to not participate" nothing within the Act will apply to you.

What doesn't make sense is how our representatives, all the attorneys and the experts who have studied it for years cannot read and understand that everyone has the right to not participate. Does it make sense to you. It made me read Section 1555 over and over to see if I was reading it correctly. It blew my mind when I first read it. Did it blow your mind?

Michael Vandeburg

CHAPTER 2

UNDER NO DUTY TO ACT

Obamacare creates the perception that everyone is required by law to carry a minimum amount of health insurance. But, I ask the question what law compels someone to a duty to act? I mean what law makes someone have a duty to buy insurance? According to the law that is what is takes to make someone legally buy insurance according to the penalties section. Let us read it:

Page 321
15 "CHAPTER 48—MAINTENANCE OF
16 MINIMUM ESSENTIAL COVERAGE
"Sec. 5000A. Requirement to maintain minimum essential coverage.
17 "SEC. 5000A. REQUIREMENT TO MAINTAIN MINIMUM ESSEN
18 TIAL COVERAGE.

Page 336
3 "(g) ADMINISTRATION AND PROCEDURE.—

4 "(1) IN GENERAL.—The penalty provided by this
5 section shall be paid upon notice and demand by the
6 Secretary, and except as provided in paragraph (2),
7 shall be assessed and collected in the same manner as
8 an assessable penalty under **subchapter B of chapter**
9 **68.**
10 "(2) SPECIAL RULES.—Notwithstanding any
11 other provision of law—
12 "(A) WAIVER OF CRIMINAL PENALTIES.—In
13 the case of any failure by a taxpayer to timely
14 pay any penalty imposed by this section, such
15 taxpayer shall not be subject to any criminal
16 prosecution or penalty with respect to such fail
17 ure.

If you read the statutes above you can see that enforcement of the penalties are implemented by subchapter B of chapter 68. I would like to point out that on page 321 that Chapter 48 has been added to the Internal Revenue Code of 1986. Even though they do not state what title chapter 68 comes from, it does appear to be Title 26. I guess you have to be a mind reader to figure it out, very confusing to even me. It is very frustrating trying to figure out this pile of garbage in the first place. If you look below this section is being added to Title 26, Internal Revenue code.

Page 321
12 (b) IN GENERAL.—Subtitle D of the Internal Revenue
13 Code of 1986 is amended by adding at the end the following
14 new chapter:
15 **"CHAPTER 48—MAINTENANCE OF**
16 **MINIMUM ESSENTIAL COVERAGE**

On a side note, our government is going to be very sorry they every tied this to Title 26, because of the 1939 Statutes at Large, "existing rights and liabilities" will trump it. If Obamacare interferes with any "right" or "liability" contained in the 1939 Statutes at Large it will over-ride it by right. And just so happens I have written 4 books on the 1939 Statutes at Large. You can start laughing now, because there is a freight train coming down the tracks, and there isn't going to be much left of Obamacare by the time I'm through, just saying!!! It's picking up steam; throw a little more coal on the fire boys. In actuality, chapter one and two will take it down without using the 1939 Statutes at Large.

Let us read chapter 68 definitions:

> TITLE 26 - INTERNAL REVENUE CODE
> Subtitle F - Procedure and Administration
> CHAPTER 68 - ADDITIONS TO THE TAX, ADDITIONAL AMOUNTS, AND ASSESSABLE PENALTIES
> Subchapter B - Assessable Penalties
> PART I - GENERAL PROVISIONS
> Sec. 6671. Rules for application of assessable penalties
> (a) Penalty assessed as tax
> The penalties and liabilities provided by this subchapter shall be paid upon notice and demand by the Secretary, and shall be assessed and collected in the same manner as taxes. Except as otherwise provided, any reference in this title to "tax" imposed by this title shall be deemed also to refer to the penalties and liabilities provided by this subchapter.
> (b) Person defined
> The term "person", as used in this subchapter, includes an officer or employee of a corporation, or a member or employee of a partnership, who as such officer, employee, or member <u>is under a duty to perform the act in respect of which the violation occurs.</u>

In my opinion since Obamacare has been determined by the Supreme Court to be a tax, there is in no way that they can ever prove that an individual, employee, natural person, business, corporation, or someone living on Mars, is under any "duty to perform the act". No one has a duty to act. I want someone to prove that I owe a penalty, or must buy insurance because I am under a "duty to act". There is no duty, just a suggestion to buy or not to buy. The government's legal argument will be that you are under a duty to act because we have a gun to your head. Is that why our government is buying so much ammunition to shoot us if we don't buy mandated health insurance? Either way it is a personal choice to buy or not to buy, not a duty to act.

What is a "duty to act" or "failure to act"? Here are some example quotes:

> "In **personal injury** and other **tort** cases, the phrase "duty to act" may refer to one of two things. First, people generally have a duty to act with **reasonable care** to prevent harm. If a person fails to do so, he may be liable for **negligence.** More often, however, the phrase "duty to act" means that a person has a duty to do a specific thing, and that if he fails to do it, he may be liable for failure to act."

> "Also, negligence law does not usually impose a duty to rescue or defend someone else, as long as the would-be rescuer did not cause the danger. Even if a bystander realizes another person is in danger, the bystander generally does not have a duty to rescue that person and cannot therefore be held liable if the bystander chooses not to act."

> "Like the standard duty to act, however, a duty to act to rescue or defend someone does exist if the person in danger and the rescuer or defender have a certain type of relationship toward one another."

> "Duty of a party to take necessary action to prevent harm to another party or the general public. Breach of duty to act may make a party liable for damages, depending on the circumstances and relationship between the parties." http://www.rotlaw.com/legal-library/what-is-a-duty-to-act-what-is-failure-to-act/

CHAPTER 3

RIGHT OF EXEMPTION IF YOU CANNOT AFFORD COVERAGE

The following section allows you to not pay any penalties for not having coverage. I will also point out that my opinion is that the "in general" section is expansive in its meaning. That means it isn't limited to this outline. How can the government say who can afford it and who cannot afford it? That should be left to every "natural person" to determine for their household if they can afford it or not. No government has that right, period! Wars have been fought over much less, and it appears that our oppressive government is constantly picking a fight, like school yard thugs stealing our lunch money every day.

Page 321
15 *"CHAPTER 48—MAINTENANCE OF*
16 *MINIMUM ESSENTIAL COVERAGE*
''Sec. 5000A. Requirement to maintain minimum essential coverage.
17 *"SEC. 5000A. REQUIREMENT TO MAINTAIN MINIMUM ESSEN*
18 *TIAL COVERAGE.*

19 *"(a) REQUIREMENT TO MAINTAIN MINIMUM ESSEN*
20*TIAL COVERAGE.—An applicable individual shall for each*
21 *month beginning after 2013 ensure that the individual, and*
22 *any dependent of the individual who is an applicable indi*
23*vidual, is covered under minimum essential coverage for*
24 *such month.*

Page 328
22 "(e) EXEMPTIONS.—No penalty shall be imposed
23 under subsection (a) with respect to—
24 "(1) INDIVIDUALS WHO CANNOT AFFORD COV
25 ERAGE.—

Page 329
1 "(A) **IN GENERAL**.—Any applicable indi
2 vidual for any month if the applicable individ
3 ual's required contribution (determined on an
4 annual basis) for coverage for the month exceeds
5 8 percent of such individual's household income
6 for the taxable year described in section
7 1412(b)(1)(B) of the Patient Protection and Af
8 fordable Care Act. For purposes of applying this
9 subparagraph, the taxpayer's household income
10 shall be increased by any exclusion from gross
11 income for any portion of the required contribu
12 tion made through a salary reduction arrange
13 ment.
14 "(B) REQUIRED CONTRIBUTION.—For pur
15 poses of this paragraph, the term 'required con
16 tribution' means—
17 "(i) in the case of an individual eligi
18 ble to purchase minimum essential coverage
19 consisting of coverage through an eligible
20 employer-sponsored plan, the portion of the
21 annual premium which would be paid by
22 the individual (without regard to whether
23 paid through salary reduction or otherwise)

24 for self-only coverage, or

Page 330
1 ''(ii) in the case of an individual eligi
2 ble only to purchase minimum essential
3 coverage described in subsection (f)(1)(C),
4 the annual premium for the lowest cost
5 bronze plan available in the individual
6 market through the Exchange in the State
7 in the rating area in which the individual
8 resides (without regard to whether the indi
9 vidual purchased a qualified health plan
10 through the Exchange), reduced by the
11 amount of the credit allowable under section
12 36B for the taxable year (determined as if
13 the individual was covered by a qualified
14 health plan offered through the Exchange for
15 the entire taxable year).

I would claim your right to not pay a penalty based on your facts that you cannot afford it. If they want to challenge you, tell them let's go to court. It doesn't matter if you had a million dollars in the bank, that it is your right to determine if you can afford it or not, based upon your own opinion.

Your legal argument should be that "In General" is expansive in its meaning, not limiting to the governments definition. I would state facts that you live in the real world and have bills to pay, a food bill, clothes to buy, rent to pay, electricity bills, child support, alimony to pay, and on and on it could go. The real world is broke, and the biggest reason you are broke is because our government keeps shoveling their pile of crap upon you, and not living within their means, like the real world has to live within its means!!!

Every jury should be sympathetic to your right to determine your own personal finances, and your claim not being able to afford it. Except those who are looking for a free ride and no personal responsibility. Here is an excerpt from my book, "Income Tax Fraud: Know Your Rights and Liabilities". It will help you understand terms:

<u>"When reading terms, first, they establish a set boundary or limits for a term, second, they define the definition of the term, and third, once inside the definition of the term or meaning, they then become expansive to include everything within the definition</u>. There are people and court cases that argue both sides to the definition of "includes or including" to be either "limiting or expansive." They are both right, as it is first limiting and then expansive. Take a look at this court case from the 1939 Statutes at Large era:

"Although Section 526(f) defines "Transferee" to <u>include</u> "donee, heir, legatee, devisee, and distributee," those are not, by express command of the statute, the only meanings to be attributed to "transferee" for Section 1111(b) [currently numbered Section 7701(c)] specifies that **<u>"includes" shall not be deemed to exclude other things otherwise within the meaning of the term defined</u>**. It has been held, we think correctly, that these words of inclusion were not intended to limit the meaning of the word "transferee," but to eliminate any doubt as to the inclusion of the four classes specifically mentioned." *Fidelity Trust Co. v. C.I.R.*, 141 F.2d 54, 57 (#rd Cir. 1944). (Emphasis and explanation added.)

Let us use a simple term to illustrate my point of view. From dictionary.com, the term is "cow:"

(1) Cow.— The term "cow" means a large hoofed mammal *(Equus caballus)* having a short-haired coat, a long mane, and a long tail, domesticated since ancient times and used for riding and for drawing or carrying loads; an adult male horse; a stallion.

It is obvious that the meaning of cow has nothing to do with the word cow as we know it. The term "cow" is defined as a horse, of course. No cows, as we know them to be, fall within the meaning of the term "cow" as defined. Now, the meaning of cow would be expansive to all breeds of horses. If one had a miniature horse or even a mule, one would be roped into the term "cow."

Likewise, the IRS first writes you a letter telling you to pay the tax on your "cows." You get mad and write a letter back stating that they are mules not "cows" within the definition of the term cow. The IRS writes you a letter back stating that your position is frivolous, and yes, they are "cows" according to the law. You get madder than hell and write another letter and so forth until off to court you go.

Most mule owners would probably challenge the law that their mules are not "cows" and are not within the definition of cows or horses and should not be taxed. The Judge determines that there is nothing exempting the mule within the law, and since it takes a horse to make a mule it is 50 percent horse; therefore, it is a "cow" by definition and you will pay the tax.

I hope this makes sense to you. What becomes confusing is when one cannot get a clear picture or definition of the meaning. Then you apply part (a):

> (a) <u>When used in this title, where not otherwise distinctly expressed or manifestly incompatible with the intent thereof-</u>

I ask the question, who determines what is manifestly incompatible with the intent thereof? When you cannot tell by reading the statutes what the "term" is meaning or implying, then one uses the standard title meanings of the *"terms."* All chapters and sections that don't have defined *"terms"* within them will use the *"standard terms"* of this title.

In my personal opinion, the whole title is unconstitutional due to vagueness. Judges cannot even tell you the true meanings of these laws. This is the main reason as to why our government is so intent on it remaining that way, because it is a cash cow! Mmmmoooooooooowwwww."

CHAPTER 4

TERM EMPLOYEE BY RIGHT ONLY CORPORATE PERSONS

There is only one section in the Act that defines the term "Employee", Sec. 6002, page 1513. It links 42 U.S.C. Section 1877(h)(2) for the definition of employee. It is important to legally enforce Obamacare, it must have all terms defined. Otherwise, it is a fraud. If you are wondering what links this definition of employee to the other sections in question is page 351, (6) OTHER DEFINITIONS.

Page 307
12 ''(2) FULL-TIME EQUIVALENT EMPLOYEES.—
13 ''(A) IN GENERAL.—The term 'full-time
14 equivalent employees' means a number of em
15 ployees equal to the number determined by divid
16 ing—
17 ''(i) the total number of hours of serv
18 ice for which wages were paid by the em

19 ployer to employees during the taxable year,
20 by
21 ''(ii) 2,080.

Page 350
14 ''(4) FULL-TIME EMPLOYEE.—
15 ''(A) IN GENERAL.—The term 'full-time em
16 ployee' means an employee who is employed on
17 average at least 30 hours of service per week.
18 ''(B) HOURS OF SERVICE.—The Secretary,
19 in consultation with the Secretary of Labor,
20 shall prescribe such regulations, rules, and guid
21 ance as may be necessary to determine the hours
22 of service of an employee, including rules for the
23 application of this paragraph to employees who
24 are not compensated on an hourly basis.

Page 351
15 ''(6) OTHER DEFINITIONS.—Any term used in
16 this section which is also used in the Patient Protec
17 tion and Affordable Care Act shall have the same
18 meaning as when used in such Act.

Page 1513
13 **SEC. 6002. TRANSPARENCY REPORTS AND REPORTING OF**
14 **PHYSICIAN OWNERSHIP OR INVESTMENT IN**
15 **TERESTS.**
16 Part A of title XI of the Social Security Act (42 U.S.C.
17 1301 et seq.) is amended by inserting after section 1128F
18 the following new section:

Page 1530
18 ''(7) EMPLOYEE.—The term 'employee' has the
19 meaning given such term in **section 1877(h)(2)**.

Now when you read the Social Security Act it defines employee relationships under common law. That alone would be impossible to defeat in court if you were challenging it. What is important is the connection of Obamacare to Title 42 and Title 26 as you can read below:

> Sec. 1877. **[42 U.S.C. 1395]** (a) Prohibition of Certain Referrals.—
> (h) Definitions and Special Rules.—For purposes of this section:
> (2) Employee.—An individual is considered to be "employed by" or an "employee" of an entity if the individual would be considered to be an employee of the entity <u>under the usual common law rules applicable in determining the employer-employee relationship</u> (as applied for purposes of section 3121(d)(2) of the Internal Revenue Code of 1986).

Now you're wondering where am I going with this discussion. In the 1939 Statutes at Large Congress created *"unambiguously conferred rights and liabilities"*. What does that mean? It means any taxation right or liability created by Congress in 1939 is "supreme law" over any other taxation statute written after 1939. It becomes a clear violation of your *Statutory Federal Rights* under "color of law", which is a clear violation of the United States Congress "<u>unambiguous conferred rights and liabilities</u>" per the 1939 Statutes at Large:

> U.S.C. TITLE 26, Subtitle F, CHAPTER 80, Sec. 7851
> (b) Effect of repeal of Internal Revenue Code of 1939
> **(1) <u>Existing rights and liabilities</u>**
> The repeal of any provision of the Internal Revenue Code of 1939 shall not affect any act done or any right accruing or accrued, or any suit or proceeding had or commenced in any civil cause, before such repeal; **<u>but all rights and liabilities under such code shall continue, and may be enforced in the same manner, as if such repeal had not been made.</u>**

Why is this important? Because the original Social Security statutes are part of the 1939 Statutes at Large; and within those statutes is a key that unlocks a door that will apply another layer of death to Obamacare. Read it and weep, Obama.

SEC. 1426. DEFINITIONS.
When used in this subchapter—

(a) **WAGES**.—The term "wages" means all remuneration for employment, including the cash value of all remuneration paid in any medium other than cash; except that such term shall not include that part of the remuneration which, <u>after remuneration equal to $3,000 has been paid to an individual by an employer with respect to employment</u> during any calendar year, is paid to such individual by such employer <u>with respect to employment</u> during such calendar year.

(b) **EMPLOYMENT**.—The <u>term "employment" means any service of whatever nature</u>, performed <u>within the United States by an *employee* for his employer</u>, except— (Ref. Statute for exemptions).

(c) **EMPLOYEE**.—<u>The term "employee" includes an officer of a corporation.</u>

SEC. 1607. DEFINITIONS.
<u>When used in this subchapter—</u>

(a) **EMPLOYER**.—The term "employer" does not include any person unless on each of some twenty days during the taxable year, each day being in a different calendar week, the total number of individuals who were in his employ for some portion of the day (whether or not at the same moment of time) was eight or more.

(b) **WAGES**.—The term "wages" <u>means all remuneration for employment</u>, including the cash value of all remuneration paid in any medium other than cash.

(c) **EMPLOYMENT**.—The term "employment" means any service, of whatever nature, performed <u>within the United States</u> by an employee for his employer, except—

(h) **EMPLOYEE**.—The term "employee" <u>includes an officer of a corporation.</u>

It is very clear to read the definition of the term "Employee" within chapter 9, sections 1426 and 1607 of the employment taxes chapter and see that the defined "meaning" does not include "persons", "individuals", or "natural persons". The defined "meaning" per Congress only states "officers of a corporation". This evidence more than proves that the Social Security Taxes by "right" does not apply to any "non-corporate officer" citizen "within" or "without" the term "United States".

That means that there isn't any authority to force any corporation to pay a penalty for all employees outside of this definition of "employee" by right. Once a corporation claims their rights it will definitely make it hard to fund Obamacare. I would say impossible. Here is what most attorneys say and think:

> "Somewhere along the line, someone will make a similar argument based on not finding a legal definition for the English language article "the". Now you and I recognize this as a frivolous argument based on a ridiculous conclusion. However, it is useful in describing the issue at hand. Many definitions and uses of language in law, do not require specific definition because they are derivative of other sources and recognized by the reasonable person for their true meaning; they are only contested by those that are looking for a loop hole or a way to deflect its meaning from self." Expert Attorney, Ed Johnson

Sounds like Bill Clinton arguing the meaning of the word "is". It is OK for attorneys to argue the meaning of words, but if a citizen does it they are label a protestor immediately. Is there any wonder why our government is so oppressive when we have the majority of the attorneys in America bowing down to whatever our government says? They don't fight for our rights, it's yes sir, Uncle Sam. I ask all attorneys, at what point is it OK to question our government about their over taxing us? Is it 4 trillion a year, 5 trillion a year, 6 trillion a year, 7 trillion a year, 8 trillion a year in taxes? At what point will the American people have the right to say to our government that you are taxing us to death, and when will we have the right to protest? Tell me, because I want to know. Frankly, I am sick to death of everyone looking down their self-righteous nose and trying to belittle anyone who protests our government about their taxation abuses. Whether you like it or not, everyone in this country enjoys their freedom based upon our forefathers protesting tyrants. Every generation has a _God-given duty_ to protest all tyrants in government.

Only an idiot would pay a tax that he does not owe. And only an idiot wouldn't try to find a way out of paying a tax that he does not owe. And only an idiot wouldn't question our government at every turn.

A good story comes to mind. I am eating at a restaurant with my cousin. I order a Philly Cheese Steak sandwich, except I don't want the mushrooms that come on it. The waiter comes over and takes our order. Now here comes the miss communication. I ask, "I don't want the mushrooms, can I replace them with extra onions?"

No comment as the waiter writes down my order. The problem! Here comes the check and it has a dollar on it for the extra onions. My cousin asks me, "Did you ordered something extra?" "No!" I replied.

Would you say something about it? My cousin didn't want me to say anything about it. But, I got mad about it and asked to have the dollar removed. The waiter comes back and tells me that the owner will not remove the dollar. I say, "OK, I will never come back to this restaurant again." I messed up! I should of demanded those mushrooms I left off my sandwich before I left. Instead the restaurant profited my dollar and the mushrooms I left off my sandwich. I should of refused and told them to call the police.

The point, we have the right to not be ripped off of our hard earned property by President Obama and our Congress. And we have the right to speak up, demand our rights, and stop paying for all these **"extra onions"** just because President Obama says we have too.

President Obama, you're a liar and a thief. Congress, you're a liar and a thief. So take your **"extra onions"** and stick them where the sun doesn't shine. By the way, the poor waiter got no tip.

CHAPTER 5

BY RIGHT PENALTIES ONLY APPLY TO CORPORATE PERSONS

By right the United States Congress exempted "natural persons" from the Income Tax Penalty Statutes in the 1939 Statutes at Large. I submit these facts to support my belief that Congress exempted all "natural person's" from Income Tax Penalties:

> **1939 Statutes at Large, Subtitle A, <u>Chapter 1-INCOME TAX</u>**
> Subchapter C, Supplement D-Returns and Payment of Tax
> **SEC. 145. Penalties.**
> (a) FAILURE TO FILE RETURNS, SUBMIT INFORMATION, OR PAY TAX.-<u>Any person required under this chapter</u> to pay any tax, or required by law or regulations made under authority thereof to make a return, keep any records, or supply any information, for the purposes of the computation, assessment, or collection of any tax <u>imposed by this chapter</u>, who willfully fails to pay such tax, make such return, keep such records, or supply such information, at the time or times required by law or regulations, shall, in addition to other penalties provided by law, be guilty of

a misdemeanor and, upon conviction thereof, be fined not more than $10,000, or imprisoned for not more than one year, or both, together with the costs of prosecution.

(b) FAILURE TO COLLECT AND PAY OVER TAX, OR ATTEMPT TO DEFEAT OR EVADE TAX.-Any person required <u>under this chapter</u> to collect, account for, and pay over any tax imposed <u>by this chapter</u>, who willfully fails to collect or truthfully account for and pay over such tax, and any person who willfully attempts in any manner to evade or defeat any tax imposed by this chapter or the payment thereof, shall, in addition to other penalties provided by law, be guilty of a felony and, upon conviction thereof, be fined not more than $10,000, or imprisoned for not more than five years, or both, together with the costs of prosecution.

(c) **PERSON DEFINED**.-The term "<u>person</u>" as used in this section <u>includes an officer or employee of a corporation or a member or employee of a partnership, who as such officer, employee, or member is under a duty to perform the act in respect of which the violation occurs</u>.

The <u>Income Tax chapter 1</u> per "unambiguous conferred rights" does not apply penalties to "natural persons." This deception is a fraud by the United States Government and the Internal Revenue Service. Congress never gave any authority to the United States Government to prosecute any "natural person" in the 50 united States. They only have the right to apply a penalty to someone who is under a duty to perform an act in respect of which the violation occurs. Funny that the definition is still the same as our current code.

CHAPTER 6

STATES CLAIM RIGHT OF "FREEDOM NOT TO PARTICIPATE"

Let me see if I can rip another one out of the ballpark. Can it be legally claimed that States are nonprofit entities? They are setup to represent the citizens of that State. They are definitely not in the business of making a profit, especially California and Michigan. The ball is floating in the water folks!!! Vandeburg is rounding third again, and heading for home. Looks like the Jackasses are calling the bullpen! Obama's scratching his head over this one folks.

It looks like the Jackasses are bringing Hillary out of the bullpen. She is warming up folks. Her first pitch is that States are public-sector entities and are therefore disqualified. Well that was a good fast ball! Didn't think she had it in her arm. OK, then, if the Obamacare is forcing all the States to provide Medicaid for Obamacare health care plans are they therefore now legally classified as an issuer of mandated healthcare plans? Yes, is my opinion! They should qualify for the "Freedom not to Participate" under the provision exemption of health insurance issuer.

21 **Subtitle G—Miscellaneous**
22 **Provisions**

Page 362
16 **SEC. 1555. FREEDOM NOT TO PARTICIPATE IN FEDERAL**
17 **HEALTH INSURANCE PROGRAMS.**
18 <u>**No individual, company, business, nonprofit entity**</u>, or
19 health insurance issuer offering group or individual health
20 insurance coverage <u>**shall be required to participate**</u> in any
21 Federal health insurance program created under this Act
22 (<u>**or any amendments made by this Act**</u>), or in any Federal
23 health insurance program expanded by this Act (<u>**or any**</u>
24 <u>**such amendments**</u>), and there shall be no penalty or fine

Page 363
1 imposed upon any such issuer for choosing not to partici
2 pate in such programs.

What are eligible entities per Obamacare? Let's see if Hillary really threw a fastball.

Page 45
1 Subtitle B—Immediate Actions to
2 Preserve and Expand Coverage
3 SEC. 1101. IMMEDIATE ACCESS TO INSURANCE FOR UNIN
4 SURED INDIVIDUALS WITH A PREEXISTING
5 CONDITION.

Page 45
13 (1) IN GENERAL.—The Secretary may carry out
14 the program under this section directly or through
15 contracts to eligible entities.

16 <u>(2) ELIGIBLE ENTITIES.—To be eligible for a</u>
17 <u>contract under paragraph (1), an entity shall—</u>
18 <u>(A) be a State or nonprofit private entity;</u>

19 (B) submit to the Secretary an application

20 at such time, in such manner, and containing
21 such information as the Secretary may require;
22 and
23 (C) agree to utilize contract funding to es
24 tablish and administer a qualified high risk pool
25 for eligible individuals.

It appears to me that by Section 1101 (b)(2), States are qualified entities because the exemption is for nonprofit entities, and it does not state that only nonprofit (private) entities are eligible for exemptions. If you read the statutes below you will see that States are also mandated to set up pools of health insurance for individuals. It is my opinion that States are qualified under both set statutory conditions: Nonprofit Entities and Health Insurance Issuer. These sections are what gives states the right to opt out of everything.

Page 46
1 (3) MAINTENANCE OF EFFORT.—To be eligible to
2 enter into a contract with the Secretary under this
3 subsection, a State shall agree not to reduce the an
4 nual amount the State expended for the operation of
5 one or more State high risk pools during the year pre
6 ceding the year in which such contract is entered into.
7 (c) QUALIFIED HIGH RISK POOL.—
8 (1) IN GENERAL.—Amounts made available
9 under this section shall be used to establish a quail
10 fied high risk pool that meets the requirements of
11 paragraph (2).
12 (2) REQUIREMENTS.—A qualified high risk pool
13 meets the requirements of this paragraph if such
14 pool—
15 (A) provides to all eligible individuals
16 health insurance coverage that does not impose
17 any preexisting condition exclusion with respect
18 to such coverage;
19 (B) provides health insurance coverage—

20 (i) in which the issuer's share of the
21 total allowed costs of benefits provided
22 under such coverage is not less than 65 per
23 cent of such costs; and
24 (ii) that has an out of pocket limit not
25 greater than the applicable amount de

Page 47
1 scribed in section 223(c)(2) of the Internal
2 Revenue Code of 1986 for the year involved,
3 except that the Secretary may modify such
4 limit if necessary to ensure the pool meets
5 the actuarial value limit under clause (i);
6 (C) ensures that with respect to the pre
7 mium rate charged for health insurance coverage
8 offered to eligible individuals through the high
9 risk pool, such rate shall—
10 (i) except as provided in clause (ii),
11 vary only as provided for under section
12 2701 of the Public Health Service Act (as
13 amended by this Act and notwithstanding
14 the date on which such amendments take ef
15 fect);
16 (ii) vary on the basis of age by a factor
17 of not greater than 4 to 1; and
18 (iii) be established at a standard rate
19 for a standard population; and
20 (D) meets any other requirements deter
21 mined appropriate by the Secretary.
22 (d) ELIGIBLE INDIVIDUAL.—An individual shall be
23 deemed to be an eligible individual for purposes of this sec
24 tion if such individual—

Page 48
1 (1) is a citizen or national of the United States
2 or is lawfully present in the United States (as deter

3 mined in accordance with section 1411);
4 (2) has not been covered under creditable cov
5 erage (as defined in section 2701(c)(1) of the Public
6 Health Service Act as in effect on the date of enact
7 ment of this Act) during the 6-month period prior to
8 the date on which such individual is applying for
9 coverage through the high risk pool; and
10 (3) has a pre-existing condition, as determined
11 in a manner consistent with guidance issued by the
12 Secretary.

Michael Vandeburg

CHAPTER 7

CLAIM RIGHT OF "TAX EXEMPT STATUS"

This loophole applies to both businesses and individuals. Under the 1939 Statutes at Large, Congress exempted most corporations, and the majority of citizens are exempt through section 4 special classes of taxpayers. It defines your liabilities for the income tax. If you read my 2 books, Income Tax Fraud: Know Your Rights and Liabilities, and Corporate Income Tax: Claim Your Right to Zero Tax Liability, you will know if you can claim your tax exemption per statute. The point is if you're not liable for filing a tax return by exemption per statutes, then you are not liable to file a return for Obamacare. It is debatable if it would hold up in court do to our government's possible argument that it is a separate return and not part of the income tax return.

You are probably wondering if my income tax books are true. The real problem is that no one seems to read any of the statutes; everyone takes the government's word as truth, instead reading it and questioning them. I really question all the supposedly healthcare experts that have been looking at Obamacare for several years, and they can't find anything to destroy it??? Well, I've been looking at it for about 4 weeks and found several major issues within the Obamacare statutes, not including the 1939 Statutes at Large issues. Are the attorneys and accountants complicit in allowing a fraud to be perpetrated upon Americans, or are our reasoning skills completely in the sewer??? Obviously, all these attorneys that read it received no reasoning skills in college. Or is it just another opportunity for attorneys and accountants to fleece Americans???

In the 1939 Statutes at Large Congress created *"unambiguously conferred rights and liabilities"*. What does that mean? It means any taxation right or liability created by Congress in 1939 is "supreme law" over any other taxation statute written after 1939. It becomes a clear violation of your statutory federal rights under "color of law", which is a clear violation of the United States Congress "<u>unambiguous conferred rights and liabilities</u>" per the 1939 Statutes at Large:

> U.S.C. TITLE 26, Subtitle F, CHAPTER 80, Sec. 7851
> (b) Effect of repeal of Internal Revenue Code of 1939
> **(1) Existing rights and liabilities**
> The repeal of any provision of the Internal Revenue Code of 1939 shall not affect any act done or any right accruing or accrued, or any suit or proceeding had or commenced in any civil cause, before such repeal; <u>**but all rights and liabilities under such code shall continue, and may be enforced in the same manner, as if such repeal had not been made.**</u>

Why is this important to Corporations? Because in the 1939 Congress exempted the majority of Corporations from the income tax! That liability exemption can be claimed, and enforced. The only reason this Obamacare claim might not hold up in court would be due to the fact that the government might claim that this return is different than an Income Tax Return. Regardless, read my books and claim your rights to exemption for Income Taxes. There are also exemptions that can be claimed by Individuals, and "natural persons". Each book is only $20, cheap considering I spent 5 years studying and pondering it, and another 3 or 4 years writing about it. It can be all yours for only $40!!! Now that is a bargain. The rewards for America will be an economy and a people that can enjoy their freedom and liberty from a tyrannical oppressive government.

Page 353
13 **SEC. 1514. REPORTING OF EMPLOYER HEALTH INSURANCE**
14 **COVERAGE.**
15 (a) IN GENERAL.—Subpart D of part III of subchapter
16 A of chapter 61 of the Internal Revenue Code of 1986, as
17 added by section 1502, is amended by inserting after section
18 6055 the following new section:
19 **"SEC. 6056. LARGE EMPLOYERS REQUIRED TO REPORT ON**
20 **HEALTH INSURANCE COVERAGE.**
21 "(a) IN GENERAL.—Every applicable large employer
22 required to meet the requirements of section 4980H with
23 respect to its full-time employees during a calendar year
24 shall, at such time as the Secretary may prescribe, make
25 a return described in subsection (b).

Page 354
1 "(b) FORM AND MANNER OF RETURN.—A return is de
2 scribed in this subsection if such return—
3 "(1) is in such form as the Secretary may pre
4 scribe, and
5 "(2) contains—
6 "(A) the name, date, and employer identi
7 fication number of the employer,
8 "(B) a certification as to whether the em
9 ployer offers to its full-time employees (and their
10 dependents) the opportunity to enroll in min
11 imum essential coverage under an eligible em
12 ployer-sponsored plan (as defined in section
13 5000A(f)(2)),
14 "(C) if the employer certifies that the em
15 ployer did offer to its full-time employees (and

16 their dependents) the opportunity to so enroll—
17 ''(i) the length of any waiting period
18 (as defined in section 2701(b)(4) of the Pub
19 lic Health Service Act) with respect to such
20 coverage,
21 ''(ii) the months during the calendar
22 year for which coverage under the plan was
23 available,

Page 355
1 ''(iii) the monthly premium for the
2 lowest cost option in each of the enrollment
3 categories under the plan, and
4 ''(iv) the applicable large employer's
5 share of the total allowed costs of benefits
6 provided under the plan,
7 ''(D) the number of full-time employees for
8 each month during the calendar year,
9 ''(E) the name, address, and TIN of each
10 full-time employee during the calendar year and
11 the months (if any) during which such employee
12 (and any dependents) were covered under any
13 such health benefits plans, and
14 ''(F) such other information as the Sec
15 retary may require.

CHAPTER 8

CONSTITUTIONAL ISSUES

Let us count the ways to take this pile horse crap down. I was just talking to a co-worker about this very subject. All of the attorneys and politicians are either completely idiots, or just utterly incompetent and they all need to resign yesterday. Their incompetence is making me look like a freaking genius, but the question needs to be asked, are they idiots, or is Obamacare a conspiracy by both parties to reduce the middle class to nothing, enslaving everyone under the government's boot? What happened to the Tea Party Representatives? Can no one in Washington read and inform the citizens about their rights?

My answer, after weighing all the facts within the Obamacare statutes, and especially after reading Section 1555, is that they are both idiots and a conspiracy. How can it be said that after 3 years that someone hasn't informed the masses that they can simply claim their right of "Freedom Not the Participate"??? Has no one is Washington read it by now??? Nancy said, "We have to pass it to know what is inside it!" Well, it's been 3 years and has no one still read it, is that your excuse??? Or is the truth that our representatives are too stupid to read???

Here is a list of some constitutional issues that should have been argued in court by now? It makes me wonder why these issues have not been argued in court. These following four issues are excerpts from my book, "Income Tax Fraud: Know Your Rights and Liabilities", I am not going to rewrite them for Obamacare, but the picture should be clear that they apply to Obamacare since the Supreme Court ruled that it is just a tax.

I. Evidence of the Current written United States Tax Laws violate the "Equal Protection Clause" determining that all Men are to be Treated Equally, and are Unconstitutional.

The current written Tax Laws violate the United States Constitution, which established an "Equal Protection Clause" determining that all men are to be treated equally:

> **AMENDMENT XIV**
> Passed by Congress June 13, 1866. Ratified July 9, 1868 Section 1. All persons born or naturalized in the United States, and subject to the jurisdiction thereof, are citizens of the United States and of the State wherein they reside. No State shall make or enforce any law which shall abridge the privileges or immunities of citizens of the United States; nor shall any State deprive any person of life, liberty, or property, without due process of law; nor to deny to any person within its jurisdiction the *equal protection of the laws*.

The current written Tax Laws that favor one group of citizens above another group of citizens or written Tax Laws that favor one group of citizens exemptions above another group of citizens also violates this clause. (Example: Different tax brackets for the level of income). In the *United States v. Butler* (1936), the Supreme Court stated:

> "A tax, in the general understanding of the term, and as used in the Constitution, signifies an exaction for the support of the government. The word has never been thought to connote the expropriation of money from one group for the benefit of another."

Written Tax Laws that select single individuals or corporations and give them special exemption laws makes them the subject of capricious legislative favor and lacks the semblance of legitimate tax legislation which violates the established "Equal Protection Clause" determining that all men are created equal:

> "Cooley, in his treatise on Taxation (2d Ed. 215), justly [157 U.S. 429, 596] observes that 'it is difficult to conceive of a justifiable exemption law which should select single individuals or corporations, or single articles of property, and, taking them out of the class to which they belong, make them the subject of capricious legislative favor. Such favoritism could make no pretense to equality; it would lack the semblance of legitimate tax legislation.' " *Pollock v. Farmers' Loan & Trust Co., 157 U.S. 429 (1895).*

Writing Tax Laws that discriminate between those of different levels of income violates the established "Equal Protection Clause" determining that all men are created equal:

> "<u>The income tax law under consideration is marked by discriminating features which affect the whole law. It discriminates between those who receive an income of $4,000 and those who do not. It thus vitiates, in my judgment, by this arbitrary discrimination, the whole legislation.</u> Hamilton says in one of his papers (the Continentalist): 'The genius of liberty reprobates everything arbitrary or discretionary in taxation. It exacts that every man, by a definite and general rule, should know what proportion of his property the state demands; whatever liberty we may boast of in theory, it cannot exist in fact while [arbitrary] assessments continue.' 1 Hamilton's Works (Ed. 1885) 270. The legislation, in the discrimination it makes, is

class legislation. Whenever a distinction is made in the burdens a law imposes or in the benefits it confers on any citizens by reason of their birth, or wealth, or religion, it is class legislation, and leads inevitably to oppression and abuses, and to general unrest and disturbance in society. It was hoped and believed that the great amendments to the constitution which followed the late Civil War had rendered such legislation impossible for all future time. But the objectionable legislation reappears in the act under consideration. It is the same in essential character as that of the English income statute of 1691, which taxed Protestants at a certain rate, Catholics, as a class, at double the rate of Protestants, and Jews at another and separate rate. Under wise and constitutional legislation, every citizen should contribute his proportion, however small the sum, to the support of the government, and it is no kindness to urge any of our citizens to escape from that obligation. If he contributes the smallest mite of his earnings to that purpose, he will have a greater regard for the government and more self-respect [157 U.S. 429, 597] for himself, feeling that, though he is poor in fact, he is not a pauper of his government. And it is to be hoped that, whatever woes and embarrassments may betide our people, they may never lose their manliness and self-respect. Those qualities preserved, they will ultimately triumph over all reverses of fortune." *Pollock v. Farmers' Loan & Trust Co., 157 U.S. 429 (1895).*

II. Evidence of the Current written United States Tax Laws violate the "Due Process Clause" determining that all Men are Guaranteed Due Process, and are Unconstitutional.

Written United States Tax Laws that discriminate between those who are married and unmarried violates the "Due Process Clause" of the Fifth Amendment:

Brushaber v. Union Pacific Railroad Co., 240 U.S. 1 (1916). "1. The statute levies one tax called a normal tax on all incomes of individuals up to $20,000 and from that amount up by gradations, a progressively increasing tax called an additional tax, is imposed. No tax, however, is levied upon incomes of unmarried individuals amounting to $3,000 or less nor upon incomes of married persons amounting to $4,000 or less. The progressive tax and the exempted amounts, it is said, are based on wealth alone and the tax is therefore repugnant to the due process clause of the Fifth Amendment."

"It is true that it is elaborately insisted that although there be no express constitutional provision prohibiting it, the progressive feature of the tax causes it to transcend the conception of all taxation and to be a mere arbitrary abuse of power which must be treated as wanting in due process."

III. Evidence of the Current written United States Tax Laws violate the "Expenditure Clauses," and are Unconstitutional.

Congress violates the spending of tax dollars on unconstitutional activities, thus making the Taxing Unconstitutional. (Examples: Giving tax dollars to foreign governments all around the world. Giving money to the benefit of one class of citizens, called welfare. Government subsidies for abortions, etc...):

"Let the expenditure be to promote the general welfare, still it is needful in order to insure its use for the intended purpose to influence any action which Congress cannot command because within the sphere of state government, the expenditure is unconstitutional. And taxes otherwise lawfully levied are likewise unconstitutional if they are appropriated to the expenditure whose incident is condemned." *U.S. v. Butler, 297 U.S. 1 (1936).*

IV. Evidence of the Current written United States Tax Laws and their enforcement creates a "CLEAR AND PRESENT DANGER" to the economic survival of the 50 united States, and are Unconstitutional.

"Clear and Present Danger doctrine. Doctrine in constitutional law, first formulated in *Schenck v. U.S., 249 U.S. 47, 39 S.Ct. 247, 63 L.Ed. 470*, providing that governmental restrictions on First Amendment freedoms of speech and press will be upheld if necessary to prevent grave and immediate danger to interests which government may lawfully protect." Black's Law Dictionary 6th Edition.

> "Speech which incites to unlawful action falls outside the protection of the First Amendment where there is direct connection between the speech and violation of the law; this is the "clear and present danger test." " *People v. Winston, 64 Misc.2d 150, 314 N.Y.S.2d 489, 495.*

Our current legislation presents a "Clear and Present Danger" to the right of everyone to pursue life, liberty, property and the pursuit of happiness and to all of our individual rights, freedoms, and protections; therefore, it should be deemed unconstitutional. When our legislation presents a "Clear and Present Danger" to incite unlawful action in which Congress is supposed to protect us against, it should be struck down. The current taxation legislation is a "Clear and Present Danger" to the destruction of our nation. Congress has crossed the line from helping the general welfare and is pursuing a taxation policy of destruction to our liberties and our nation.

Our current taxation policies and our treasury policies, and the Unconstitutional Federal Reserve Bank is embarking upon a path or road to economic destruction for the United States of America. This path is very well documented by many organizations and documents. The "Grandfather Reports" by far, shows the best overall picture of the road to destruction. With an overall total debt of around <u>160 Trillion Dollars</u> for our nation. The future outcome to the American way of life and freedom is certainly doomed without an outside Divine Intervention. Our forefathers understood money and taxation and the overwhelming power of taxation to destroy a nation's creativity. John Marshall stated it best:

> "Power to tax involves the power to destroy;...the power to destroy may defeat and render useless the power to create."

It is clear that our political parties and representatives are on a **"Death Ride"** for America and they have no plans or intentions of stopping. Why else would Congress and Obama pass the National Defense Authorization Act? Does Congress and our President need to power to lock Americans away for life, with no due process?

This new interpretation of the doctrine "Clear and Present Danger" has never been present to our courts before, but its meaning is well founded throughout our history and deeply rooted in our traditions and way of life. Such as, that it is also understood foundational in the American concept of Constitutional liberty. If the right is found to be a fundamental liberty interest under this "deeply rooted" constitutional test, statutes or other government actions that infringe upon the fundamental foundation and fabric of our nation are presumptively invalid and subject to exceedingly strict scrutiny. This "Clear and Present Danger" violation applies interchangeably to both the States, via the Fourteenth Amendment's Due Process Clause, and to the federal government, via the Fifth Amendment's Due Process Clause. It prohibits the federal government from depriving any person of life, liberty, or property without due process of law.

If the Supreme Court wants to uphold the right of Congress and our President to destroy our nation, then, by all means they can start paying for it first. It will be time for the Supreme Court to hand over all their possessions to help pay for our debts. It will be time for the Supreme Court to put **"ALL"** their own property and money where your "Legalese Mouths Are"!!!

Michael Vandeburg

CHAPTER 9

WHAT SHOULD I DO?

My opinion is that I would learn my 1939 Rights and Liabilities and claim them, that is what I would do! No sense in paying Income Taxes if the statutes exempt you. But if nothing else, I would write these words on your Income Tax Return.

Option 1:

"I claim my Right of "Freedom Not to Participate" in Obamacare, per Section 1555! All laws of Patient Protection and Affordable Care Act do not Apply to my household."

Option 2:

"I claim my Right of "Freedom Not to Participate" in Obamacare, per Section 1555. I also claim my Right of "Under No Duty to Act" by Obamacare, per Title 26, Subtitle F, Chapter 68(b). All laws of Patient Protection and Affordable Care Act do not Apply to my household."

Option 3:

"I claim my Right of "Freedom Not to Participate" in Obamacare, per Section 1555. I also claim my Right of "Under No Duty to Act" by Obamacare, per Title 26, Subtitle F, Chapter 68(b). All laws of Patient Protection and Affordable Care Act do not Apply to my household. I also claim my right of exemption per Chapter 48, Section 5000e determining "in general" that my household cannot afford this overpriced healthcare insurance."

Option 4:

"I claim my Right of "Freedom Not to Participate" in Obamacare, per Section 1555. I also claim my Right of "Under No Duty to Act" by Obamacare, per Title 26, Subtitle F, Chapter 68, Section 6671(b). All laws of Patient Protection and Affordable Care Act do not Apply to my household. I also claim my right of exemption per Chapter 48, Section 5000e determining "in general" that my household cannot afford this overpriced healthcare insurance. The term employee and penalties by right only applies to Corporate Persons and does not apply to my household per 1939 Statutes at Large, Sec. 1426, Sec. 1607, TITLE 26, Subtitle F, CHAPTER 80, Sec. 7851, "Existing Rights and Liabilities", and Title 26, Chapter 68, Section 6671(b)."

Feel free to add some of the other issues to your statement. I only used five of the issues in my options. If the IRS harasses you, I would file a Title 42, Section 1983, lawsuit under color of law.

What about buying my old insurance policy?

First, I would call your insurance provider and state that you are claiming your right of exemption so you can legally buy your old policy from them.

Second, if that doesn't work I would use these two options to write a certified mailed letter to your insurance provider stating that you have a legal right to purchase your old policy because you claimed your right of exemption. State to them that they have a legal right to sell your old policy to you. If they deny you that right I would suggest a lawsuit per Title 42, Section 1983, under color of law.

Also state, Barrack Obama has established legal precedence supporting the fact that individuals and companies can be exempted per Section 1555 of Obamacare. Otherwise; the Courts need to rule that Obama has abused his power and has no right to exempt anyone. As it stands Congress has no problem with Obama exempting all individuals and companies because he isn't violating the law per Section 1555 of Obamacare.

I hope this book has enlightened everyone to their Obamacare rights. May God bless you and your family.

Michael Vandeburg

www.ingramcontent.com/pod-product-compliance
Lightning Source LLC
Chambersburg PA
CBHW071807170526
45167CB00003B/1207